indian cooking
made easy

by Jan Purser and Ajoy Joshi

Quick, easy and delicious recipes to make at home.

PERIPLUS

Contents

MAIL ORDER SOURCES

Finding the ingredients for Asian home cooking has become very simple. Most supermarkets carry staples such as soy sauce, fresh ginger and lemongrass. Almost every large metropolitan area has Asian markets serving the local population—just check your local business directory. With the Internet, exotic Asian ingredients and cooking utensils can be easily found online. The following list is a good starting point of online merchants offering a wide variety of goods and services.

http://www.asiafoods.com
http://store.Indianfoodsco.com
http://www.orientalpantry.com/
http://www.zestyfoodservings.com
http://asianwok.com/
http://www.indiangrocerynet.com/

Introduction

As a young boy growing up in Hyderabad (India) in the early 1960s, I dreamt of eating in the Taj Mahal Hotel restaurants, famous for their crispy Masala Dosai—rice flour pancakes with a yummy filling (page 38-41). My school was behind one of the restaurants, and passing it daily was the beginning of my love not only for Masala Dosai but for food in general.

After I finished my schooling, many paths were open to me, but I decided that I had to do something different. Hence I began the challenging but rewarding journey to become a cook. During my catering school days in Madras, I was fortunate to work at the Taj Coramandel and Fisherman's Cove Hotels, the former as a waiter (providing the tips that sustained me financially) and the latter as a trainee cook (giving me the tips I needed to become a chef). The next step was very clear—I had to become a chef.

Working at the Taj Group of hotels, especially in the banquet kitchen as a sous-chef, was always exciting. Once the food was cooked, it was displayed attractively, which brought out my artistic instincts. After hard work, and more hard work, I realized my dream in 1988, when I was appointed executive chef of the Gateway Hotel in Bangalore. This also opened up opportunities for me to explore other parts of the world and take my cooking skills overseas.

Thirteen years and six restaurants later, I am at Nilgiri's in Sydney, discovering my roots and cooking Indian food with a simple philosophy guided by the famous Hyderabadi saying that good food comes with *fursat* (leisure) and *mohabbat* (love). The food at Nilgiri's is simple, and the menu small, which allows the chefs to focus on the finer details of each dish.

Cooking Indian food, like any other great cuisine, is a celebration of life. The recipes in this book are a selection of popular and notable dishes, presented in a format that makes them easy to prepare. I hope that you enjoy the journey of cooking each dish as much as the pleasure of eating it. Finally, as any self-respecting Indian would say at the conclusion of a good meal, Anha Datha Sukhi Bhava—"May the provider of this food be happy and content."

—Ajoy Joshi

Basic Indian Ingredients

Ajwain seeds are tiny seeds that have the flavor of thyme with peppery overtones. Similar in appearance to celery seeds, they are used in Indian breads, fried snacks, lentil and vegetable dishes.

Asafoetida is a pungent yellow powder produced from the dried gum of a giant fennel plant. When added in small amounts to food, it offers a mild onion or garlic flavor—a fact that caught the attention of Hindu Brahmins and Jains whose diets do not allow the use of onions and garlic.

Banana leaves are used to wrap foods before steaming or baking them. Cut the leafy part away from the center vein and pass it over a gas flame or briefly scald with boiling water in a tub or basin until it turns bright green and softens, making folding easier. Aluminum foil or parchment (baking) paper can be substituted.

Basmati rice is the long grain rice used throughout India. This rice has a delightful fragrance when cooked and complements Indian food. Once cooked, the rice grains should be separated and flaky.

Black lentils, also known as urad dal or black gram, are sold whole or split. When the outer hull is removed, they appear creamy white and are known as black gram dal. They are also ground into split black lentil flour (urad flour). They are quite small compared with other lentils and cook more quickly. The split lentils become mushy when cooked. Black lentils are used in vegetable dishes, and are roasted to add a nutty flavor to some dishes. The flour is combined with rice flour in dishes such as dosai.

Cardamom pods are whole green or brown pods filled with fragrant, tiny black seeds. For the best flavor, grind your own just before using. In this book, the pods are usually ground fresh for each recipe. You can also buy ground cardamom powder, but the flavor is not as rich. Cardamom is a key ingredient in garam masala and many other spice mixes, and is used in numerous Indian dishes.

the flavor is similar and garbanzo beans make a good substitute. Yellow split peas may also be substituted, although the flavor will differ somewhat and they take a little longer to cook. Split chickpeas are used in soups, snacks and vegetable dishes, and sometimes in desserts.

used throughout India and generally added just before serving a dish to add a fresh accent. It is sold in bunches and has dark green serrated leaves and thin stems. Chop the leaves and some of the stems when a recipe calls for chopped cilantro as the stems also add flavor.

Chickpea flour is made from dried chickpeas that are ground to a fine yellow flour rich in protein and dietary fiber. Also known as *besan* or gram flour, it is used in many Indian dishes, both sweet and savory. The flour has a slightly nutty flavor and is often used as an ingredient in batters, pastries and doughs.

Chili peppers come in many varieties and we generally use a combination of small red and green fresh Thai serrano or bird's-eye chilies in this book. Don't remove the seeds, just chop the chilies finely or grind to a paste in a small food processor. If you prefer less heat, remove the seeds and white membranes before chopping or grinding. Or, reduce the number of chilies used in the recipe.

Coconut milk and **coconut cream** are produced by mashing freshly grated coconut meat with water and then squeezing and straining the mixture to extract the liquid. Coconut cream is obtained by adding less water (about $^1/_2$ cup/125 ml to the grated flesh of 1 coconut) whereas coconut milk has more water added (about 1 cup/250 ml per coconut). Coconut cream and milk are now readily available in cans and paper carton packets. Dilute the cream with equal amounts of water to obtain milk.

Chickpeas, known in India as channa dal or gram lentils, are smaller than the garbanzo beans used in Western cookings although

Cilantro or coriander leaves is a flavored herb

Coconuts should be reasonably fresh and heavy for their size, and when shaken, the juice audibly sloshes around inside. The coconut flesh, once removed from the shell, should be creamy white in color, crisp, firm and fiberous with a pleasant coconut flavor. Avoid old coconuts that are dried out with very little juice inside.

Cumin seeds are from a plant in the parsley family. Briefly dry-roasting the seeds brings out their flavor, which is earthy, pungent and a little bitter. Used whole or ground, cumin seeds are a common ingredient in spice mixes, curries and raitas. Black cumin seeds have a slightly less bitter flavor.

Dried chilies called for in these recipes are dried Asian serrano chilies unless specified otherwise. Don't deseed them. If you prefer less heat, decrease the number of chilies used.

Dried mango powder, also know as *amchoor*, is used to give a tart tang to many Indian dishes. It is ground from dried unripe mangoes. If it is not available, a squeeze of lemon juice makes an acceptable substitute.

Coriander seeds are usually dry-roasted in a skillet before being ground alone or as part of a spice mix. Freshly ground coriander seeds have a fragrance that is lemony and herbaceous and much richer than ground coriander powder.

Curry leaves are native to India and Sri Lanka, and are predominantly used in the south. They have a strong flavor with a hint of citrus. The dark-green shiny leaves resemble small bay leaves and grow on a small tree to roughly half a finger length. Curry leaves are used in sauces, spice mixes, marinades, salads and soups. You can use dried curry leaves as a substitute, but the fresh leaves are more fragrant.

Fennel seeds are used whole or ground, and contribute an aniseed-like flavor to meat and vegetable dishes, desserts, pickles and chutneys. They are sometimes added to garam masala spice mixes. Whole fennel seeds, plain or sugar coated, are served at the end of a meal as a digestive aid.

Fenugreek seeds are roasted to bring out their bitter, sharp and nutty flavor. They are added to spice mixes, breads, chutneys and lentil dishes. If you cannot find the seeds, use ground fenugreek powder.

Green-brown lentils are sometimes sold as brown or green lentils and yet are one and the same. They are generally sold whole, not split. Green-brown lentils are a little larger than other lentils, have a slightly nutty flavor and hold their shape when cooked.

Indian bay leaves come from the cassia tree. They are larger and have a slightly sweeter flavor than European bay leaves. Dried bay leaves are used in spice mixes, and in some meat and rice dishes from the north.

Jaggery is dark brown sugar made from sugarcane juice. It has a flavor resembling brown sugar with molasses added. Dark brown sugar may be substituted although the flavor is not be quite the same.

Mace is the red outer coating of the nutmeg seed, with a more pungent flavor. Blade mace is the whole coating, which has been removed from the nutmeg seed and dried. It has a coarse, netted appearance and goes well in pulaos and seafood dishes (see photo for Nutmeg below).

Mangoes are eaten in India while still unripe, or when ripe. Green or unripe mangoes are made into pickles and chutneys and are used to add a tartness to savory dishes. The sweet, juicy ripe mangoes are enjoyed raw or made into ice cream or lassi yoghurt drinks.

Mustard seeds come in two varieties—black and brown, and both are called for in this book. They are always lightly fried in hot oil for a few seconds to release their pungent flavor before other ingredients are added. Mustard oil is a popular cooking oil in India and is simply oil that has been infused with the fragrant of lightly fried mustard seeds.

Nigella seeds, also known as *kalonji*, are tiny black seeds sometimes incorrectly referred to as black cumin or onion seeds, although they are not related to onions. The seeds have a flavor similar to cumin but with a slightly bitter, metallic edge. They are used in breads, salads and lentil dishes, and with vegetables. If you cannot find them, substitute cumin seeds or ground cumin.

Nutmeg is the seed of a tree which is ground and most commonly used in desserts in India. It is also used as an ingredient in some spice mixes for savory dishes. Its mild, sweet flavor complements both white and red meats. The spice is thought to help tenderize meat.

Paprika is made from red peppers that are dried and ground to produce a powder that is used to flavor and add color to savory dishes. Paprika is available in various heat levels; mild forms, with the flavor of bell pepper (capsicum), are used in this book.

Peppercorns are "the king of spices," and feature extensively in Indian cooking. Both whole black peppercorns and ground white peppercorns are used in this book. Always grind peppercorns just before adding to a dish to ensure the best aroma and flavor.

Rice flour is milled from uncooked rice grains. Medium to coarse rice flour is used to make Dosai, the fermented rice pancakes popular in Southern India. Finer rice flour is used in *idli*, the little steamed cakes served with lentils, often for breakfast. The finer rice flour is also used in batters and some desserts.

Saffron threads are the dried stigmas from a variety of crocus flower, each of which produces only three stigmas. Harvesting saffron is labor-instensive, making it the most costly spice in the world. Saffron threads are generally soaked in a warm liquid to release their intense gold-yellow color and pungent, earthy aroma and flavor.

Semolina flour is made from durum wheat. It has a bland flavor and slightly coarse texture. Coarse semolina is used in the recipes in this book, and makes a crunchy coating on fried dishes although a finer semolina may be substituted. Semolina, both coarse and fine, is used in Indian sweets and some breads.

Star anise is the dried star-shaped seed pod from a variety of magnolia tree. Commonly used in Chinese cooking, star anise also makes an appearance in Indian dishes. Its flavor is similar to that of aniseed, but has more depth of flavor and sweetness.

Turmeric is an essential ingredient in many Indian dishes and lends a deep gold color and sharp, sometimes slightly bitter flavor. It comes from the root of a tropical plant and is generally dried and then ground, though it is also available fresh.

Yellow split peas are small lentils which have many names—including toor dal, toovar dal, arhar dal and pigeon peas. They are commonly used in vegetarian dishes and soups. Smaller than split chickpeas, they have a mild, slightly sweet flavor and tend to become mushy when cooked.

Tamarind concentrate, also called tamarind paste, is made from the pulp of the tamarind tree. It is simply spooned from the jar without the need for any preparation, and adds a tart, fruity flavor to savory dishes. It is available in jars in supermarkets. If you prefer using dried tamarind pulp, then mix the amount called for in the recipe with an equal amount of water, mash and strain to obtain a thick juice.

Vegetable oil and **melted unsalted butter** is an ideal substitute for the butter oil or ghee that is commonly used in Indian cooking. Ghee is also widely available canned, but a combination of vegetable oil with melted butter works as well or better. If making several dishes that call for it, mix a quantity of melted butter and oil at a ratio of 50:50 so that the mixture is ready to measure out as needed. The combination of butter and oil offers a higher burning point with a similar flavor to ghee.

Garam Masala Spice Blend

This roasted spice mix is used in lots of different Indian recipes and you can buy it already blended and ground in most Indian food shops. For a richer flavor and aroma, though, it's worth buying the spices and roasting your own blend, then grinding a little bit as needed for each recipe.

1 small cinnamon stick, broken into pieces
4 teaspoons whole green cardamom pods
3 black cardamom pods
4 teaspoons whole cloves
4 teaspoons mace blades
4 teaspoons peppercorns
4 teaspoons fennel seeds
3 Indian bay leaves, torn
into quarters
1 teaspoon freshly grated nutmeg

Makes about 1/3 cup

1 Heat a small pan over low heat. Separately dry-roast the cinnamon, cardamom, cloves, mace, peppercorns, fennel seeds and bay leaves until fragrant and lightly browned. Make sure the heat is not too intense as the spices should not be blackened or burnt.

2 As each spice is roasted, place it in a bowl. Allow the roasted spices to cool. Add the freshly grated nutmeg to the mix, blend thoroughly and place in an airtight jar. Store in the refrigerator or freezer for up to 1 year.

3 Just before using the Garam Masala, grind it to a powder in a spice grinder.

4 Add the ground spice mix to the recipe as needed.

Steamed Basmati Rice

You can easily double this recipe to make enough for 4 people. It's important to rinse the rice grains well before cooking to remove excess starch; otherwise the rice can become gluey. A general guide is to soak the rice in twice its volume of water and then cook it in the soaking water. The rice must be steamed over very low heat for the last 10 minutes.

1 cup (200 g) uncooked basmati rice
2 cups (500 ml) water
$1/4$ teaspoon salt

Serves 2; makes 2 cups (200 g) cooked rice

1 Place the rice in a bowl and add cold water to cover. Swirl with your hand, let the rice settle, then drain off the water. Repeat 6-7 times. Add enough water to cover the washed rice and leave to soak for 20 minutes.
2 Drain the water from the soaked rice into a heavy saucepan with a tight-fitting lid. Add the salt and bring to a boil over medium–high heat. Add the soaked rice, stir once, then return to a boil. Reduce the heat to low and simmer, partially covered, until most of the water is absorbed, 10–15 minutes.
3 Cover, reduce the heat to very low and let the rice steam for 10 minutes. Remove from the heat and set aside for 5–10 minutes without lifting the lid.

Sambhar Masala Spice Mix

2 tablespoons coriander seeds
2 small dried chili peppers, broken into pieces
$^1/_4$ teaspoon fenugreek seeds
$^1/_4$ teaspoon mustard seeds
$^1/_3$ teaspoon cumin seeds
$^1/_4$ teaspoon ground cinnamon
1 tablespoon unsweetened dried shredded coconut
3 curry leaves

1 Heat a small pan over low heat. Dry-roast the coriander, dried chili, fenugreek, mustard seeds, cumin and cinnamon until fragrant and lightly browned. Place the roasted spices in a bowl.

2 In the same pan, dry-roast the coconut, stirring constantly, until lightly browned. Remove from the heat and add to the roasted spices. In the same manner, dry-roast the curry leaves until crisp, then add to the spices. Mix well and set aside to cool.

3 Grind all the spices to a powder in a spice grinder just before using.

Makes about 4 tablespoons

Sambhar Tomato Lentil Stew

1½ cups (300 g) split yellow lentils, rinsed and drained
8 cups (2 liters) water
1 teaspoon ground turmeric
1 lb (500 g) tomatoes (about 3–4 medium), diced, or one 16-oz (450-g) can chopped tomatoes
2 onions, chopped
3 tablespoons Sambhar Masala Spice Mix (opposite page)
18 curry leaves
2 teaspoons tamarind concentrate
1 teaspoon salt, or to taste
²/₃ cup (30 g) chopped cilantro (coriander leaves)

1 Combine the lentils, water and turmeric in a large saucepan and bring to a boil. Reduce the heat to low and cook, partially covered, until the lentils are soft and mushy, about 30 minutes. Add the chopped tomato and onion, and continue cooking, partially covered and stirring occasionally, until soft, about 30 minutes.
2 Add the Sambhar Masala, tamarind, curry leaves and salt, mix well and return to a boil. Taste and adjust the seasoning, then stir in the cilantro. Keep the stew warm over low heat, partially covered, until serving.

Serves 6-8

Herb and Ginger Yogurt Dip

1/2 teaspoon cumin seeds
1/4 cup (10 g) mint
1/4 cup (10 g) cilantro
(coriander leaves)
1 in (3 cm) fresh ginger
root, peeled and sliced
1 green chili pepper
1 1/4 cups (300 ml) plain
yogurt
1/2 onion, thinly sliced
1/2 teaspoon salt, or to
taste

1 In a small pan over low heat, dry-roast the cumin seeds until fragrant and lightly browned, taking care not to burn them. Remove from the heat and set aside to cool, then grind to a powder in a spice grinder.
2 Process the mint, cilantro, ginger and chili in a food processor until fine.
3 Whisk the yogurt in a bowl, add the onion, ground cumin and ground herb mixture, and mix well. Season with the salt.

This dip can be made 2 days ahead and stored in an airtight container in the refrigerator.

Makes 1 1/2 cups (375 ml)

Carrot Salad with Yogurt (Carrot Pachadi)

1 cup (250 ml) plain
yogurt
8 oz (250 g) carrots,
(about 2–3 medium),
peeled and grated
1/2 teaspoon salt, or to
taste
2 teaspoons oil
1/2 teaspoon mustard
seeds
1 dried red chili pepper
9 curry leaves
2 tablespoons chopped
cilantro (coriander
leaves)

1 Whisk the yogurt in a bowl, add the grated carrot and mix well. Season with the salt.
2 In a small saucepan, heat the oil over medium–low heat. Add the mustard seeds and sauté until they crackle, about 30 seconds. Stir in the chili pepper and curry leaves, and cook, stirring, for 15 seconds. Remove from the heat, add to the yogurt mixture and mix well. Sprinkle with cilantro before serving.

Carrot Pachadi can be made up to 6 hours ahead, then stored in an airtight container in the refrigerator.

Makes 2 1/2 cups

Mint Raita (Mint Yogurt Dip)

$^1/_2$ cup (20 g) mint
$^1/_2$ cup (20 g) cilantro
  (coriander leaves)
2 in (5 cm) fresh ginger
  root, peeled and sliced
1 green chili pepper
1 cup (250 ml) plain
  yogurt
$^1/_2$ teaspoon salt, or to
  taste

1 Process the mint, cilantro, ginger and chili in a food processor until fine.
2 Whisk the yogurt in a bowl, add the mint mixture and mix well. Season with the salt.

Raitas are based on yogurt, which is whipped or whisked. You can use either whole-milk or reduced-fat yogurt. This can be made 1 day ahead and stored in an airtight container in the refrigerator.

Makes $1^1/_2$ cups (375 ml)

Cucumber Yogurt Dip (Cucumber Raita)

$1^1/_2$ teaspoons cumin
  seeds
1 cup (250 ml) plain
  yogurt
1 baby cucumber, finely
  chopped
Salt and freshly ground
  black pepper, to taste
$^1/_4$ cup (10 g) chopped
  cilantro (coriander
  leaves)

1 In a small pan over low heat, dry-roast the cumin seeds until fragrant and lightly browned, taking care not to burn them. Remove from the heat and set aside to cool, then grind to a powder in a spice grinder.
2 Whisk the yogurt in a bowl. Stir in the cucumber and ground cumin, and season with salt and pepper. Add the cilantro and mix well.

This raita can be made up to 6 hours ahead and stored in an airtight container in the refrigerator.

Makes $1^1/_2$ cups

Fresh Coconut Chutney

1 whole fresh coconut
1/2 cup (20 g) chopped
  cilantro (coriander
  leaves) with stems
1-2 green chili peppers,
  chopped
2¹/₂ teaspoons grated
  fresh ginger root

1 teaspoon salt, or to taste
3–4 tablespoons water
  (optional)
2 teaspoons oil
1¹/₂ teaspoons mustard
  seeds
18 curry leaves, coarsely
  chopped

Chutney can be made
1 day ahead and stored
in an airtight container
in the refrigerator.

Makes 3¹/₂ cups

1 To open the coconut, carefully pierce the "eyes" with a thick metal skewer or other pointed object. Drain the coconut water into a cup. Taste it to make sure it is sweet and not off (keep the water for drinking as it is highly nutritious).

2 Use a hammer to crack the coconut open. Turn the pieces shell-side up and use the hammer to break them into small pieces, then use a small, sharp knife to pry the coconut meat from the shells. Peel the outer brown skin from the meat.

3 Process the coconut meat in a food processor until coarsely chopped. Add the cilantro, chili, ginger and salt, and continue processing until all the ingredients are fine, adding 3–4 tablespoons of water if necessary. Transfer to a bowl.

4 In a small pan, heat the oil and stir-fry the mustard seeds over medium heat until they crackle, about 30 seconds. Remove from the heat, stir in the curry leaves, and then combine with the coconut mixture and mix well.

Date and Tamarind Chutney

8 oz (250 g) pitted dried dates
$3/4$ cup (185 ml) white vinegar
$1/3$ cup (60 g) jaggery or dark brown sugar
$1/4$ cup (60 ml) oil
3 tablespoons salt
$2^1/2$ tablespoons tamarind concentrate
2 tablespoons ground red pepper

1 cinnamon stick, broken into pieces
2 teaspoons green cardamom pods
2 teaspoons whole cloves

Mango Spice Mix
$1/2$ teaspoon ground coriander seeds
$1/4$ teaspoon ground cumin
2 teaspoons Garam Masala (page 10)

$1/2$ teaspoon dried mango powder or 1 tablespoon freshly squeezed lemon juice

Bottled chutney will keep for up to 1 year in a cool cupboard. After opening, store it in the refrigerator for up to 6 months.

Makes $1^1/2$ cups

1 Prepare the Mango Spice Mix by combining all the ingredients and mixing well.
2 In a large saucepan, combine all the ingredients except the Spice Mix and bring to a boil, stirring. Reduce the heat to low, cover the pan partially and simmer, stirring constantly, until the dates are soft, 35–45 minutes. Remove from the heat and stir in the Spice Mix. Spoon into a clean glass jar, cover tightly and set aside to cool. Store in a cool cupboard for at least 1 week before using.

Potato Samosas

Oil, for deep-frying

Pastry
2 1/3 cups (350 g) flour,
  sifted
Salt, to taste
3 tablespoons melted
  butter
3/4 cup (185 ml) warm
  water

Filling
4 teaspoons oil
1 1/2 teaspoons cumin
  seeds
1 teaspoon grated fresh
  ginger root
1 lb (500 g) potatoes
  (about 3–4 medium),
  boiled whole, peeled
  and coarsely mashed
1/2 teaspoon ground red
  pepper

1 small green chili, finely
  chopped
1 tablespoon chopped
  cilantro (coriander
  leaves) with stems
2 teaspoons Mango
  Spice Mix (page 17)
Freshly squeezed juice of
  1 lemon
1 teaspoon salt, or to taste

Makes 12 Samosas

1 Make the Pastry first by combining the flour and salt in a mixing bowl. Add the butter and mix well. Gradually pour in the warm water, a little at a time, and knead the mixture into a smooth dough. Wrap the dough in a plastic wrap or cover with a clean cloth and set aside for 20 minutes.

2 Prepare the Mango Spice Mix following the instructions on page 17.

3 To make the Filling, heat the oil in a wok over medium heat and stir-fry the cumin seeds until fragrant. Add the ginger, mashed potato, ground pepper and chili, and stir-fry for 3 minutes. Stir in the cilantro and Mango Spice Mix, and season with the lemon juice and salt. Remove from the heat and set aside to cool.

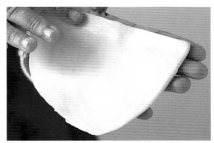

4 Divide the dough into 6 equal portions. Shape each portion into an oval and roll it out on a lightly floured surface until the oval is about 9 in (23 cm) long and $5^1/_2$ in (14 cm) wide. Cut each oval in half.

5 Place one half-oval on your hand with the straight edge aligned with your index finger. Wet a finger of the other hand and run it along the straight edge to moisten.

6 Using the other hand, fold both ends in to form a cone. Press the overlapping edges to seal them.

7 Hold the cone open and spoon $^1/_2$ of the Filling into the cone, then use a wet finger to moisten the inside edge of the dough at the open end. Pinch the edges together to seal and enclose the Filling.

8 Place the Samosa on a lightly floured baking sheet. Continue to make the other Samosas with the remaining ingredients in the same manner.

9 Fill a wok with oil to a depth of 5 in ($12^1/_2$ cm) and heat over medium heat to 375 °F (190 °C). Handling a few at a time, deep-fry the Samosas, turning often, for 3–4 minutes each until crispy and golden brown. Remove from the heat and drain on paper towels. Serve immediately.

Mixed Vegetable Pakoras

Oil, for deep-frying
1 red bell pepper, deseeded and diced
1 medium potato, peeled and diced
1 large onion, diced
1 large Asian eggplant or medium globe eggplant, diced
1 portion Mint Raita (page 15), to serve

Batter
$2^2/_3$ cups (400 g) chickpea flour
1 teaspoon whole ajwain seeds
$^1/_2$ teaspoon ground red pepper
$1^1/_2$ teaspoons salt, or to taste
4 teaspoons oil
About $1^1/_4$ cups (300 ml) water

1 Prepare the Mint Raita following the instructions on page 15. Transfer to a serving bowl and set aside.
2 To make the Batter, combine the flour, ajwain seeds, red pepper and salt in a bowl and mix well. In a small pan, heat the oil until it begins to smoke, then quickly stir it into the flour mixture. Add enough water and mix to form a thick, smooth batter.
3 Fill a wok with oil to a depth of 3 in (8 cm and heat over medium heat to 375 °F (190 °C). Meanwhile, add all the diced vegetables to the Batter and mix well. Spoon 1 heaped tablespoon of the Batter and carefully drop it into the hot oil. Deep-fry the Pakora, turning often, until golden brown on all sides, 3–4 minutes. Remove from the pan and drain on paper towels. Continue to deep-fry the remaining Batter in the same manner. Serve the Pakoras immediately with a bowl of Mint Raita on the side.

Instead of dicing the vegetables, you can cut them into thin slices, dip them in the Batter and then deep-fry until golden brown.

Makes 28 Pakoras

Chickpea Vadai

1 1/2 cups (300 g) split chickpeas or garbanzo beans
1 onion, chopped
1 tablespoon chopped cilantro (coriander leaves) with stems
2 teaspoons grated fresh ginger root
2 teaspoons crushed garlic
1-2 green chili peppers, finely chopped
4 teaspoons fennel seeds
1 1/2 teaspoons cumin seeds
18 curry leaves, finely chopped
1 teaspoon salt, or to taste
Oil, for deep-frying
1 portion Mint Raita (page 15) or Cucumber Raita (page 15), to serve

Makes 22 Vadai

1 In a bowl, combine the chickpeas with enough hot water to cover and soak for 2 hours. Drain the beans and reserve 1 cup (250 ml) of the soaking water.
2 Prepare the Mint or Cucumber Raita following the instructions on page 15. Transfer to a serving bowl and set aside.
3 Grind the soaked chickpeas to a smooth, thick paste in a food processor, adding 1–2 tablespoons of the soaking water if necessary. Add the chopped onion, cilantro, ginger, garlic, chili, fennel, cumin, curry leaves and salt, and continue to process until well combined. Transfer the ground mixture to a bowl.
4 To shape the Vadai, spoon 2 tablespoons of the ground mixture and roll it into a ball, then lightly flatten it into a patty with your palm. Place the patty on a baking sheet. Continue to shape the remaining ground mixture in the same manner.
5 Fill a wok with oil to a depth of 3 in (8 cm) and heat it over medium heat to 375 °F (190 °C). Handling a few at a time, deep-fry the patties until golden brown, 1–2 minutes on each side. Remove from the heat and drain on paper towels. Serve immediately with a bowl of Mint or Cucumber Raita on the side.

Rasam Tomato Lentil Stew

1 cup (220 g) split yellow lentils
3¹/₂ cups (875 ml) water
1 teaspoon ground turmeric
1 tablespoon oil
3 ripe medium tomatoes, coarsely chopped
1¹/₂ teaspoons tamarind concentrate
2 teaspoons crushed garlic
1¹/₂ tablespoons Spice Mix (see below)
¹/₃ cup (15 g) chopped cilantro (coriander leaves)
18 curry leaves, torn into small pieces
Freshly squeezed juice of ¹/₂ lemon
1 teaspoon salt, or to taste

Spice Mix
1 teaspoon coriander seeds
1 dried chili pepper, broken into small pieces
1 teaspoon cumin seeds
¹/₄ teaspoon mustard seeds
¹/₄ teaspoon peppercorns
4 curry leaves

1 Place the lentils in a sieve, rinse under cold running water and drain well.
2 To make the Spice Mix, heat a small pan over low heat and dry-roast all the ingredients until fragrant and lightly browned. Remove from the heat and set aside to cool. Grind the roasted spice mixture to a powder in a spice grinder.
3 Combine the lentils, water, turmeric and oil in a large, heavy saucepan, and bring to a boil over high heat. Reduce the heat to medium and simmer uncovered for about 30 minutes until the lentils are soft.
4 Add the chopped tomato, tamarind and garlic and continue to simmer uncovered for another 20–25 minutes, until the tomato breaks down. Stir in 1¹/₂ tablespoons of the Spice Mix, cilantro and curry leaves, and season with the lemon juice and salt. Remove from the heat and serve hot in individual serving bowls.

Serves 6-8

Three Lentil Stew

$^1/_2$ cup (110 g) black lentils
$^1/_2$ cup (60 g) red kidney beans
$^1/_4$ cup (50 g) split chick-peas
5 cups (1$^1/_4$ liters) water
1 cinnamon stick
3 whole cloves

3 green cardamom pods, cracked
1$^1/_2$ tablespoons finely grated fresh ginger root
1$^1/_2$ tablespoons crushed garlic
2–4 teaspoons ground red pepper

One 14-oz (440 g) can peeled tomatoes
$^2/_3$ cup (150 g) butter, chopped
Salt, to taste
4 teaspoons dried fenu-greek leaves, crushed

Serves 6

1 Rinse the lentils. Place in a large bowl with the water, cover and soak overnight.
2 Place the cinnamon, cloves and cardamom in a spice bag or wrapped in a cheese-cloth (muslin) and fasten with kitchen strings. Combine the bundle of spices, soaked lentils and water in a large saucepan and bring to a boil over medium heat. Reduce the heat to low and simmer uncovered for about 1$^1/_2$ hours, until all the lentils are tender. Add extra water if necessary to keep the lentils covered.
3 Remove and discard the spices. Add all the other ingredients except the fenugreek leaves. Increase the heat to medium and cook, stirring often, for 10 minutes. The consistency should be like a thick soup. If too thick, add a bit of water. Stir in the fenugreek leaves and remove from the heat. Serve hot with steamed rice or Paratha.

Creamy Lentils

$^2/_3$ cup (150 g) lentils
$^2/_3$ cup (150 g) yellow split peas
1 teaspoon ground turmeric
1-2 green chili peppers, halved lengthwise
1 tablespoon oil

1 teaspoon mustard seeds
1 teaspoon cumin seeds
2 teaspoons Garam Masala (page 10)
1 teaspoon ground coriander
$^1/_2$ cup (125 ml) water
3 tablespoons heavy cream

1 tomato, chopped
1 teaspoon salt, or to taste
1 tablespoon chopped cilantro (coriander leaves) with stems

Serves 6

1 Rinse the lentils and split peas, and place in a bowl. Add enough water to cover and let them soaked for 30 minutes, then drain well.

2 Bring a saucepan of water to a boil over medium heat. Add the lentils, split peas, turmeric and chili, and return to a boil. Simmer uncovered until the lentils are tender, about 30 minutes. Remove from the heat, drain, and mash coarsely.

3 Heat the oil in a wok over medium heat and stir-fry the mustard seeds until they crackle, about 30 seconds. Add the cumin, Garam Masala and coriander and stir-fry until fragrant, about 1 minute. Stir in the mashed lentil mixture, water, cream and tomato, and bring to a boil. Season with the salt, reduce the heat to low and simmer partially covered, stirring often, for about 5 minutes. Add the cilantro and remove from the heat. Serve hot.

Fragrant Basmati Tomato Rice

1 cup (200 g) uncooked basmati rice
4 cups (1 liter) water
Pinch of salt
$2^1/_2$ tablespoons oil
2 teaspoons mustard seeds
2 teaspoons split chick-peas or garbanzo beans
1 teaspoon split black lentils
1 teaspoon ground chili pepper
$^1/_2$ teaspoon ground turmeric
2 teaspoons finely grated fresh ginger root
8 curry leaves
3 ripe tomatoes, finely chopped
1 teaspoon salt, or to taste
1 tablespoon chopped cilantro (coriander leaves), to garnish

Serves 4

1 Place the rice in a bowl and add cold water to cover. Swirl with your hand, let the rice settle, then drain off the water. Repeat 6-7 times. Add enough water to cover the washed rice and leave to soak for 20 minutes.

2 Bring the water to a boil in a saucepan. Drain the soaked rice and add to the boiling water with the salt. Return to a boil and simmer, uncovered, until the rice is tender, 9–10 minutes. Do not overcook. Remove from the heat, drain in a colander and set aside.

3 Heat the oil in a wok over medium heat. Add the mustard seeds and stir-fry until they crackle, about 30 seconds. Add the chickpeas and lentils, and stir-fry until golden brown, 1–2 minutes. Add the ground pepper and turmeric, and stir-fry for 15 seconds. Stir in the ginger and curry leaves, mix well, and add the chopped tomato. Increase the heat to medium and simmer, stirring often, until the tomato is soft and the mixture thickens slightly, 5-10 minutes. Season with the salt.

4 Add the drained rice to the pan and toss gently with a large spoon to combine, taking care not to break the rice grains. Remove from the heat, sprinkle with chopped cilantro and serve immediately.

Rice is best cooked just before serving. The tomato mixture can be made several hours ahead, and then reheat before adding it to the rice.

Vegetable Pulao

1 1/2 cups (300 g) uncooked basmati rice
1/4 cup (60 ml) oil and melted butter combined
1/2 cinnamon stick
1 black cardamom pod
1 green cardamom pod
1 whole clove
1/2 blade mace
1 onion, thinly sliced
2 teaspoons finely grated fresh ginger root
2 teaspoons crushed garlic
1 teaspoon salt, or to taste
1 ripe tomato, finely chopped
1 small carrot, peeled and diced
3 oz (100 g) green beans, trimmed and sliced
1/3 cup (50 g) fresh or frozen green peas
1–2 green chili peppers, minced
2 cups (500 ml) vegetable stock, or water
1/4 cup (10 g) chopped cilantro (coriander leaves), to garnish

1 Place the rice in a bowl and add cold water to cover. Swirl with your hand, let the rice settle, then drain off the water. Repeat 6–7 times. Add enough water to cover the washed rice and leave to soak for 20 minutes.

2 Preheat the oven to 350 °F (180 °C).

3 In a large, heatproof pan, heat the oil and butter mixture over medium heat. Add the cinnamon, cardamom, cloves and mace, and sauté, stirring, until fragrant, about 30 seconds. Add the onion, ginger, garlic and salt, and continue to sauté until the onion is browned, 5–10 minutes. Stir in the chopped tomato and mix well. Add the carrot, green beans, peas and chili and sauté for about 3 minutes.

4 Drain the soaked rice and add to the pan, tossing until well combined. Pour in the stock or water and bring to a boil. Reduce the heat to low and simmer, partially covered, until most of the liquid is absorbed and steam holes appear in the mixture, about 10 minutes. Remove from the heat.

5 Cover the pan tightly with a heavy lid and bake in the oven until the rice is tender, about 10 minutes. Remove from the oven and let it stand for 10 minutes. Garnish with the cilantro and serve immediately.

Serves 4-6

Chicken Pulao

2¹/₂ cups (500 g) uncooked basmati rice
1 large onion, thinly sliced
Pinch of salt
¹/₃ cup (85 ml) oil and melted butter combined
1 cinnamon stick
1 green cardamom pod
2 whole cloves
1 star anise pod
18 curry leaves
1 small chicken (2 lbs/ 1 kg), cut into serving pieces
1 tablespoon finely grated fresh ginger root
1 tablespoon crushed garlic
1–2 green chili peppers, sliced lengthwise
³/₄ cup (185 ml) buttermilk
¹/₂ teaspoon salt, or to taste
2 ripe tomatoes, finely chopped
1 cup (250 ml) coconut milk
2¹/₂ cups (625 ml) chicken stock or water
¹/₂ cup (20 g) chopped cilantro (coriander leaves), to garnish
1 lemon, cut into wedges, to serve

1 Place the rice in a bowl and add cold water to cover. Swirl with your hand, let the rice settle, then drain off the water. Repeat 6–7 times. Add enough water to cover the rice and leave to soak for 20 minutes. In another bowl, combine the onion and salt, and mix well.

2 Preheat the oven to 425 °F (220 °C).

3 Heat the oil in a wok over medium heat and stir-fry the cinnamon, cardamom and cloves until fragrant, about 30 seconds. Stir in the star anise and ¹/₂ of the curry leaves, then add the salted onion and stir-fry until the onion is golden brown, 5–10 minutes.

4 Add the chicken pieces and stir-fry until they are light browned, about 5 minutes. Stir in the ginger, garlic, chili, remaining curry leaves and buttermilk, and season with the salt (not too much if using sea-soned stock). Simmer uncovered, turning the mixture occasionally, until the chicken is cooked through and the sauce is reduced by half (the sauce may look curdled), about 10 minutes. Add the chopped tomato, pour in the coconut milk and continue to simmer, stirring often, until the tomato is slightly soft, about 3 minutes.

5 Drain the soaked rice and add to the pan, tossing until well combined. Pour in the stock or water and bring to a boil. Simmer, partially covered, until most of the liquid is absorbed and steam holes appear in the mixture, 5–10 minutes. Remove from the heat.

6 Cover the pan tightly with a heavy lid and bake in the oven until the rice is tender, about 10 minutes. Remove from the oven and let it stand for 10 minutes. Garnish with cilantro and serve hot with lemon wedges.

Serves 8-10

Chappati (Whole Wheat Flatbreads)

2¹/₂ cups (350 g) whole
wheat flour, sifted
¹/₂ teaspoon salt
1¹/₂ tablespoons oil
1 cup (250 ml) water

Makes 6 large Chappati

The skillet must not be too hot or the Chappati will become dry. You can make the Chappati smaller if you prefer. They can be cooked several hours ahead, then reheated. Before serving, wrap them in a clean kitchen towel, then aluminum foil, and heat in a preheated oven at 225 °F (110 °C) for 5–10 minutes.

1 Combine the flour and salt in a large bowl. Make a well in the center and gradually pour in the oil and water, mixing with your hands until the mixture turns into a soft dough. Lightly knead the dough in the bowl, then cover with a damp cloth and let it stand for 20 minutes. Knead the dough on a lightly floured work surface until pliable, about 10 minutes, then cover and let it stand again for 15 minutes. Divide the dough into 6 equal portions. Shape each portion into a ball, then using a rolling pin, roll it out into a 9-in (23-cm) disk.

2 Heat a nonstick skillet over medium heat until hot. Place a Chappati on the skillet and cook, lightly pressing with a dry kitchen towel or spatula, until brown spots appear, 1–2 minutes. Turn over and cook for 1 more minute on the other side, brushing with a little oil and melted butter (optional). Remove from the heat and drain on paper towels. Continue to cook the remaining Chappati in the same manner. Serve hot with lentil stew, paneer or curry.

Poori (Puffed Fried Breads)

$2^1/_2$ cups (350 g) whole wheat flour, sifted
$^1/_2$ teaspoon salt
$2^1/_2$ tablespoons oil
1 cup (250 ml) water
Oil, for deep-frying

Poori are best cooked just before serving but the dough can be rolled out several hours in advance. Dust with flour and cover with a damp kitchen towel to keep them moist.

Makes 25 Poori

1 Combine the flour and salt in a large bowl. Make a well in the center and gradually pour in the oil and water, mixing with your hands until the mixture forms a firm dough. Knead the dough on a lightly floured work surface until pliable, about 10 minutes, then cover it with a damp cloth to avoid drying out and let it stand for 20 minutes.

2 Lightly knead the dough and divide it into 25 equal portions. Shape each portion into a ball, then using a rolling pin, roll it out to form a 5-in (13-cm) disk. Lightly dust each disk with flour and place the disks on a baking sheet, partially overlapping each other.

3 Heat the oil in a wok over medium heat to 375 °F (190 °C). Working with a few at a time, carefully slide the disks into the hot oil and keep them submerged with a spatula until they begin to puff. Deep-fry the Poori for 30–60 seconds, then turn over and continue to deep-fry the other side until golden brown. Remove from the heat and drain on paper towels. Serve immediately with a curry.

Paratha (Flaky Flatbreads)

2 1/2 cups (350 g) flour, plus a bit more for dusting, sifted
2/3 cup (100 g) whole wheat flour, sifted
Pinch of baking soda
Pinch of cream of tartar
1 teaspoon sugar
1 teaspoon salt

1/2 teaspoon nigella seeds (optional)
1 egg
3 tablespoons oil
3/4 cup (185 ml) buttermilk
3 tablespoons water
2 tablespoons melted butter, for brushing

Paratha can be rolled about 30 minutes before cooking. Keep them covered at room temperature.

Makes 12 Paratha

1 Combine the flours, baking soda, cream of tartar, sugar, salt and nigella seeds (if using) in a mixing bowl. In a small bowl, whisk the egg and oil together. Make a well in the center of the mixing bowl, gradually pour in the egg mixture, buttermilk and enough water, mixing with a wooden spoon or your hands until the mixture turns into a soft dough. Knead the dough for 10 minutes, then cover it with a damp cloth and let it stand for 15 minutes. Place the dough on a lightly floured work surface and knead for 5 more minutes until pliable, then cover, and set aside for 10 minutes.

2 Lightly knead the dough, then divide it into 12 equal portions. Roll each portion into a ball, dusting with the flour, and cover with a clean kitchen towel.

3 Using a rolling pin, roll each dough ball into a 7-in (18-cm) disk. Lightly brush the disk with the melted butter and dust with a little flour, then fold it in half. Repeat the brushing and dusting process and fold it in half again. Cover with a clean kitchen towel and set aside. Just before cooking, roll out each folded dough to about 1/8-in (3-mm) thick Paratha.

4 Heat a griddle or nonstick skillet over medium heat until hot. Place a Paratha on the pan and cook, lightly pressing with a metal spatula, until browned, 2–3 minutes. Then turn over and cook the other side, brushing with a little butter, until browned, and remove from the heat. Continue to cook all the Paratha in the same way. Serve hot.

Dosai (Rice and Lentil Pancakes)

$^3/_4$ cups (90 g) rice flour
$^1/_4$ cup (50 g) split black
   lentil flour
$^1/_2$ teaspoon salt
Water as needed

$^1/_4$ cup (60 ml) oil and
   melted butter combined

Makes 6 Dosai

1 Combine the rice flour, lentil flour and a pinch of salt in a mixing bowl. Make a well in the center and gradually pour in enough water, mixing with a wooden spoon or your hand until the mixture turns into a batter with a dropping consistency. Cover and let the batter ferment in a warm place for 12 hours or overnight.

2 Heat a griddle or nonstick skillet over high heat, spreading a thin layer of salt over the top, for 3–4 minutes, then wipe off the salt with a kitchen towel. This seasons the pan. Reduce the heat to medium and heat for 2 more minutes. To test if the temperature is right, drizzle a little oil and butter mixture on the pan, and sprinkle with water; if the water sizzles immediately on contact, the pan is ready for cooking. Wipe the pan clean.

3 Ladle $^1/_3$ cup (85 ml) of the batter onto the pan and spread it out to form a thin circle, about 7–8 in (18–20 cm) in diameter. Drizzle the Dosai with 1 teaspoon of the oil and butter mixture and fry until crispy and golden brown, 2-4 minutes.

4 Place the filling (if using) along the center and fold or roll the Dosai to cover the filling as desired. Remove from the heat and transfer the Dosai to a plate, seam side down. Continue to fry the remaining batter in the same manner.

Masala Dosai
(Rice and Lentil Pancakes with Potato Filling)

1 portion Dosai batter (pages 38-39)

$^1/_2$ portion Fresh Coconut Chutney (page 16), to serve

Potato Masala Filling

1 tablespoon oil

$^3/_4$ teaspoon mustard seeds

$^1/_2$ tablespoon split chickpeas or garbanzo beans

$^1/_2$ tablespoon split black lentils

1-2 dried chili peppers, broken into small pieces

1 teaspoon ground turmeric

9 curry leaves

1 onion, thinly sliced

$^1/_2$ teaspoon salt, or to taste

1 lb (500 g) cooked potatoes, (about 3-4), peeled and coarsely mashed

$^1/_4$ cup (10 g) chopped cilantro (coriander leaves), to garnish

1 Prepare the Fresh Coconut Chutney following the recipe on page 16.

2 To make the Potato Masala Filling, heat the oil in a wok over medium heat and stir-fry the mustard seeds until they crackle, about 30 seconds. Add the chickpeas and lentils, reduce the heat to low and stir-fry for 30 seconds, taking care not to burn them, until they are light golden brown.

3 Add the dried chili peppers and stir-fry for 15 seconds, then stir in the turmeric and curry leaves. Add the onion slices and salt, and stir-fry until the onion is translucent and fragrant, 3-5 minutes. Finally stir in the mashed potato and cilantro, and toss until well combined, 2–3 minutes. Adjust the taste with more salt if desired. Remove from the heat and set aside.

4 Make the Dosai following the instructions on pages 38-39, using one-sixth of the Potato Masala Filling for each Dosai. Serve hot with Fresh Coconut Chutney.

Cook the Dosai one at a time unless you are using a large griddle and the pancakes must be cooked just before serving. You can make the Fresh Coconut Chutney 1 day in advance.

Makes 6 Masala Dosai

Homemade Paneer Cheese

4 cups (1 liter) full cream milk

1²/₃ cups (400 ml) heavy cream

²/₃ cup (150 ml) white vinegar

Serves 4

1 Line a large, flat-bottomed sieve with a double layer of cheesecloth (muslin), allowing it to overhang from the sides of the sieve. Place the lined sieve in a large bowl. Choose a large, heavy, non-aluminum saucepan that fits inside the sieve.

2 Bring the milk slowly to a boil over medium heat in a pot. When the milk is almost boiling, stir in the cream and return to a boil again. When the milk mixture begins to boil (when it begins to bubble), pour in the vinegar, mix well and and remove from the heat. Let it stand for 2 minutes. Do not stir.

3 Using a large slotted spoon or strainer, gently lift the curds from the whey and transfer them to the lined sieve.

4 When all the curds have been transferred, gather the corners of the cheesecloth together and tie them up tightly. Then gently squeeze the wrapped paneer to extract as much of the remaining moisture as possible.

5 Leave the wrapped paneer in the sieve and place a heavy weight on top, such as the pot of whey. Set aside at room temperature until it is firm, about 25 minutes. Remove the weight from the paneer, carefully untie the cheesecloth and remove. Cut it into cubes or prepare as directed in the recipes. If not using immediately, store it in an airtight container with enough whey to cover, and keep in the refrigerator for up to 1 week.

Marinated Baked Paneer

1 portion Homemade
Paneer Cheese (opposite
page), cut into 1 x 3 in
(3 x 8 cm) chunks
$^1/_3$ cup (15 g) chopped
cilantro (coriander
leaves), to garnish
Juice of 1 lemon, to serve
Fresh greens, to serve

Marinade
1 cup (250 ml) plain
yogurt, whisked
$1^1/_2$ tablespoons finely
grated fresh ginger root
$1^1/_2$ tablespoons crushed
garlic
1-2 green chili peppers,
finely chopped

Large pinch of saffron
threads, soaked in $1^1/_2$
tablespoons hot milk
for 10 minutes
4 teaspoons oil, plus
extra oil for brushing
$^1/_2$ teaspoon salt

Serves 4

1 Preheat the oven to 475 °F (240 °C).
2 Combine the Marinade ingredients in a mixing bowl and mix well. Add the
Homemade Paneer Cheese pieces and gently mix to coat them well with the
Marinade. Set aside to marinate for about 10 minutes.
3 Lightly grease a baking sheet with a little oil and arrange the paneer pieces in a
single layer. Bake the paneer pieces in the oven, without turning, until golden
brown on their edges, about 15 minutes. Remove from the heat.
4 On serving platters, arrange the baked paneer on a bed of fresh greens, garnished
with cilantro. Drizzle with the lemon juice and serve hot.

Paneer with Spinach (Palak Paneer)

10 oz (300 g) spinach
1 1/2 teaspoons ground turmeric
2 tablespoons water
3 tablespoons oil and melted butter combined
4 teaspoons cumin seeds
2 onions, chopped
1/2 teaspoon salt, or to taste
2 tablespoons crushed coriander seeds
1 1/2 tablespoons grated fresh ginger root
1-2 green chili peppers, finely chopped
1 teaspoon ground red pepper
3 ripe tomatoes, finely chopped
1 portion Homemade Paneer Cheese (page 42), cut into 1-in (3-cm) chunks
1 teaspoon dried fenugreek leaves, to garnish
1 portion Chappati (page 34), to serve

1 Make the Chappati following the recipe on page 34.
2 Trim the spinach, wash well and placed it in a large saucepan. In a small bowl, mix 1/2 teaspoon of the turmeric with the water, and sprinkle the mixture over the spinach. Cook the spinach covered over medium heat, turning from time to time, until wilted, 3–5 minutes. Remove from the heat, drain and set aside to cool. Process the spinach in a food processor or blender until fine.
3 Heat the oil and butter mixture in a wok over medium heat and stir-fry the cumin seeds until fragrant, about 30 seconds. Add the chopped onion and salt, and stir-fry until the onion turns translucent, about 5 minutes. Stir in the remaining turmeric, coriander, ginger, chili and red pepper, and cook until fragrant, 2–3 minutes.
4 Add the chopped tomato and stir-fry for about 5 minutes until soft. Stir in the spinach and mix well. Add the paneer pieces and gently toss to coat them well with the mixture. Cook for 2-3 minutes until the paneer is warmed through. Remove from the heat, sprinkle with the fenugreek leaves and serve hot with the Chappati.

Adding turmeric to the spinach before cooking helps it retain a bright green color.

Serves 4-6

Pumpkin Kofta Balls

Oil, for deep-frying
3 tablespoons heavy
  cream
1/2 teaspoon Garam
  Masala (page 10), to
  serve

Sauce
1/4 cup (60 ml) oil
1 cinnamon stick
4 green cardamom pods
4 whole cloves
1 onion, thinly sliced
1 tablespoon finely grated
  fresh ginger root

1 tablespoon crushed
  garlic
1/2 teaspoon salt
3 teaspoons ground
  turmeric
2 teaspoons ground red
  pepper
2 ripe tomatoes, chopped
1 teaspoon honey
1 teaspoon ground mace

Pumpkin Balls
1 lb (500 g) pumpkin or
  butternut squash,
  peeled and grated

2 large potatoes, boiled,
  peeled and mashed
1/4 cup (10 g) chopped
  cilantro (coriander
  leaves)
1 tablespoon finely grated
  fresh ginger root
3 teaspoons finely
  chopped green chili
  peppers
1 teaspoon salt, or to taste
Cornstarch, for dusting

Serves 6

1 Prepare the Sauce first by heating the oil in a wok over medium heat. Stir-fry the cinnamon, cardamom and cloves until fragrant, about 30 seconds. Add the onion, ginger, garlic and salt, and stir-fry until golden brown, 3-5 minutes. Stir in the turmeric and red pepper. Add the chopped tomato and cook, stirring, until the tomato is soft, 3–4 minutes, then stir in the honey and mace. Remove from the heat and cover to keep warm.

2 To make the Pumpkin Balls, place the grated pumpkin or squash in a colander and squeeze well to extract any excess water. In a mixing bowl, combine with the mashed potato, cilantro, ginger, chili and salt, and mix well. Shape the pumpkin mixture into walnut-sized balls, and dust them with the cornstarch. Place the pumpkin balls on a baking sheet lightly dusted with cornstarch.

3 Fill a wok or saucepan with oil to a depth of 3 in (8 cm) and heat over medium heat to 375 °F (190 °C). In batches of five, gently lower the Pumpkin Balls into the hot oil and deep-fry until golden brown on all sides, 2–3 minutes. Remove from the heat and drain on paper towels.

4 Transfer the Sauce to a serving bowl and stir in the cream. Arrange the deep-fried Pumpkin Balls on serving platters, sprinkled with the Garam Masala and serve hot with the Sauce on the side.

Pumpkin Balls are best shaped and cooked close to serving time. The mixture can be made 2 hours ahead and kept at room temperature.

Mixed Vegetable Curry with Cilantro

1 fresh ear of corn or $3/4$ cup (100 g) corn kernels
1 teaspoon butter
$1^1/_2$ tablespoons oil
$1/2$ cinnamon stick
1 green cardamom pod
1 whole clove
1 onion, chopped
1 teaspoon finely grated fresh ginger root
1 teaspoon crushed garlic
$1/2$ teaspoon salt, or to taste
1 teaspoon ground red pepper
$1/2$ tablespoon crushed coriander seeds
1 teaspoon ground turmeric
1 ripe tomato, finely chopped
10 oz (300 g) button mushrooms
Freshly squeezed juice of $1/2$ lemon
2 tablespoons chopped cilantro (coriander leaves), to garnish

Serves 4

1 If using ears of corn, remove the kernels using a sharp knife. In a saucepan, melt the butter over medium heat, add the corn kernels and sauté until softened, 2–3 minutes. Remove from the heat and set aside.

2 Heat the oil in a wok over medium heat and stir-fry the cinnamon, cardamom and clove until fragrant, about 30 seconds. Add the chopped onion, ginger, garlic and salt, and stir-fry until golden brown, about 5 minutes. Stir in the red pepper, coriander and turmeric and stir-fry until fragrant, another 30 seconds.

3 Add the tomato to the pan and stir-fry for 3 minutes, until the tomato is soft. Finally add the mushrooms and corn, and cook, tossing occasionally, until the mushrooms are soft, 5–10 minutes. Season with lemon juice and more salt as needed. Remove from the heat, garnish with cilantro and serve hot.

Spicy Masala Potatoes

1 lb (500 g) potatoes (about 3–4 medium)
1 1/2 tablespoons water
1/2 teaspoon ground turmeric
1/2 teaspoon groud red pepper

2 tablespoons oil and melted butter combined
2 teaspoons cumin seeds
2 teaspoons ground coriander
1 teaspoon finely grated fresh ginger root

1 teaspoon salt, or to taste
2 tablespoons chopped cilantro (coriander leaves), to garnish
1 tablespoon freshly squeezed lemon juice

Serves 4

1 Combine the potatoes, pinch of salt and enough water to cover in a saucepan and bring to a boil over medium heat. Reduce the heat to low and simmer, partially covered, until the potatoes are tender, about 20 minutes. Remove from the heat and drain. Let the potatoes cool for 15 minutes, then peel and cube.
2 In a small bowl, combine the water, turmeric and red pepper, and mix well.
3 Heat the oil and butter mixture in a wok over medium heat and stir-fry the cumin for 30 seconds, taking care not to burn them, until fragrant. Reduce the heat to low, add the turmeric mixture and cook for 1 minute. Add the potato cubes, coriander and ginger, and toss gently until heated through and well combined, about 1 minute. Season with the salt, add the cilantro and mix well. Remove from the heat, drizzle with the lemon juice and serve hot.

Mixed Khurma Vegetables

1 1/4 cups (300 ml) water
1-2 green chili peppers,
  quartered lengthwise
9 curry leaves
1/2 teaspoon ground
  turmeric
1 potato, cut into sticks
1 carrot, cut into sticks
1 small eggplant, cut
  into sticks

1 small zucchini, cut
  into sticks
1 onion, cut into wedges
1 cup (100 g) green
  beans, trimmed and cut
  into short lengths

Yogurt Sauce
1/2 cup (125 ml) plain
  yogurt

1/2 teaspoon ground
  coriander
1/2 teaspoon ground
  cumin
1/4 teaspoon freshly
  ground black pepper
1 teaspoon salt, or to
  taste

Serves 4–6

1 Bring the water, chili, curry leaves and turmeric to a boil over medium heat in a large saucepan. Add the vegetables and mix well. Cover, reduce the heat to low and simmer, stirring occasionally, until the vegetables are just tender, about 15 minutes. Remove from the heat.

2 While cooking the vegetables, prepare the Yogurt Sauce by combining all the ingredients in a bowl and mixing well.

3 Drain off all but about 1 1/2 tablespoons of the liquid from the vegetables. Add the Yogurt Sauce to the vegetables and return to simmer over low heat, mixing gently until well combined. Do not overheat. Remove from the heat and serve hot.

Curried Green Beans

1 teaspoon ground turmeric
1 lb (500 g) green beans, trimmed and sliced
1 tablespoon oil
$^1/_2$ teaspoon mustard seeds
2 dried chili peppers
9 curry leaves
2 teaspoons finely grated fresh ginger root
1 onion, chopped
$^1/_2$ teaspoon salt
1 green chili pepper, chopped
1 tablespoon freshly squeezed lemon juice
$^1/_4$ cup (30 g) finely grated fresh coconut (optional)

1 Fill a saucepan with water and bring to a boil. Add $^1/_2$ teaspoon of the turmeric and blanch the green beans for 1–2 minutes. Remove from the heat, rinse the blanched beans under cold running water and drain well.

2 Heat the oil in a wok over medium heat and stir-fry the mustard seeds until they crackle, about 30 seconds. Add the dried chili, curry leaves and ginger, and stir-fry for 30 seconds. Stir in the onion, remaining turmeric and salt, and stir-fry until the onion is translucent, 3-5 minutes. Add the blanched beans and chili, and toss until well combined and heated through. Remove from the heat, drizzle with the lemon juice and top with the grated coconut (if using). Serve hot.

Adding turmeric to the green beans when blanching helps to intensify their green color.

Serves 4

52

Potatoes with Green Chili and Herbs

1 lb (500 g) potatoes (about 3–4 medium)
3 tablespoons oil
$^1/_2$ teaspoon mustard seeds
18 curry leaves
$^1/_2$ teaspoon ground turmeric
$^1/_2$ cup (125 ml) coconut milk
$^1/_4$ cup (10 g) chopped cilantro (coriander leaves)
1-2 green chili peppers, minced
1 teaspoon sugar
1 teaspoon salt, or to taste
Freshly squeezed juice of $^1/_2$ lemon

1 Combine the potatoes, pinch of salt and enough water to cover in a saucepan and bring to a boil over medium heat. Reduce the heat to low and simmer, partially covered, until the potatoes are tender, about 20 minutes. Remove from the heat and drain. Let the potatoes cool for 15 minutes, then peel and cube.
2 Heat the oil in a wok over medium heat and stir-fry the mustard seeds until they crackle, about 30 seconds. Add the curry leaves and stir in the turmeric, then add the potato cubes and toss gently to combine. Pour in the coconut milk, add the cilantro and chili, and season with the sugar and salt. Simmer, stirring occasionally, for about 2 minutes and remove from the heat. Drizzle with the lemon juice and serve hot.

Serves 4

Chicken Tomato Curry

1 1/2 lbs (700 g) boneless chicken thigh meat, cubed
1/3 cup (85 ml) buttermilk
3 tablespoons oil and melted butter combined
1 cinnamon stick
2 green cardamom pods, cracked
2 whole cloves
2–3 onions, chopped

2 tablespoons grated fresh ginger root
2 tablespoons crushed garlic
2 teaspoons ground red pepper
2 tablespoons ground coriander
1 tablespoon ground turmeric
4 tomatoes, diced

1 teaspoon salt, or to taste
1/3 cup (15 g) chopped cilantro (coriander leaves)
1 tablespoon crushed peppercorns
9 curry leaves

Serves 6

1 Combine the chicken and buttermilk in a large bowl and mix well. Allow to marinate for at least 15 minutes in the refrigerator.

2 Heat the oil and butter mixture in a wok over medium heat and stir-fry the cinnamon, cardamom and cloves until fragrant, about 30 seconds. Add the chopped onion, ginger and garlic and stir-fry until golden brown, 5–10 minutes. Stir in the red pepper, coriander and turmeric, and stir-fry for 1 more minute, until fragrant. Add the tomato and simmer uncovered, stirring occasionally, until the tomato is soft and the curry is slightly thickened, 10–15 minutes. Season with the salt.

3 Add the chicken and marinade to the curry and simmer half covered, stirring often, until the chicken is cooked through, 5–10 minutes. Stir in the cilantro, peppercorns and curry leaves, and remove from the heat. Serve hot with rice.

Baked Chicken with Green Chili and Herbs

1½ lbs (700 g) boneless
  chicken thigh meat,
  each halved
Oil, for greasing

Marinade
⅓ cup (15 g) chopped
  cilantro (coriander
  leaves)
¼ cup (10 g) mint
  leaves
2–3 green chili peppers,
  deseeded
1 in (3 cm) fresh ginger
  root, peeled and sliced
4 cloves garlic
1 teaspoon coarsely
  ground peppercorns
1 teaspoon salt
Freshly squeezed juice of
  1 lemon

1 To make the Marinade, grind all the ingredients, except the lemon juice, to a smooth paste in a food processor or blender, adding a little water to keep the blades moving if necessary. Transfer to a mixing bowl and stir in the lemon juice.

2 Place the chicken in the Marinade and mix until well coated. Cover and allow to marinate for at least 20 minutes.

3 Preheat the oven to 475 °F (240 °C).

4 Lightly grease a large baking sheet and arrange the marinated chicken pieces in a single layer. Bake the chicken in the oven, without turning, for 20–25 minutes until cooked through. Serve immediately.

Serves 6

Chicken with Yoghurt and Almonds

1 1/2 lbs (700 g) boneless chicken thigh meat, sliced into bite-sized pieces
1/4 cup (60 ml) oil and melted butter combined
1 1/2 onions, thinly sliced
Freshly squeezed juice of 1/2 lemon

Marinade
1 1/2 cups (375 g) plain yogurt
1 teaspoon grated fresh ginger root
1 teaspoon crushed garlic
1/2 teaspoon ground turmeric
2 teaspoons sesame seeds, ground
6 blanched almonds, ground
1 teaspoon salt, or to taste

Spice Mix
1 cinnamon stick, broken into small pieces
2 green cardamom pods
3 whole cloves
1/2 teaspoon cumin seeds

1 Combine the Marinade ingredients in a mixing bowl and mix well. Place the chicken in the Marinade and mix until well coated. Cover and allow to marinate in the refrigerator for 1 1/2 hours.
2 Prepare the Spice Mix by grinding all the spices to a powder in a spice grinder. Set aside.
3 Heat the oil and butter mixture in a wok over medium heat and stir-fry the sliced onion until golden brown, 3–5 minutes. Add the chicken with the Marinade and mix well. Reduce the heat to medium–low and simmer uncovered, turning the chicken pieces and stirring the sauce occasionally, until the chicken is cooked through, 20–25 minutes. Stir in the Spice Mix and lemon juice, mix well and simmer for 2 minutes, adjusting the taste. Remove from the heat. Serve hot with steamed rice.

Serves 6

Coconut Chicken Curry

4 teaspoons split chick-peas or garbanzo beans
4-5 dried chili peppers, broken into small pieces
3 cups (300 g) grated fresh coconut
1/4 cup (30 g) roasted unsalted peanuts or cashews
3 tablespoons oil

Serves 6

2 onions, thinly sliced
1 teaspoon salt, or to taste
1 2/3 cups (400 ml) coconut milk
3/4 cup (185 ml) water
3 lbs (1 1/3 kg) chicken, cut into 12 pieces
3/4 cup (185 ml) plain yogurt, whisked
Freshly squeezed juice of 1 lemon
4 teaspoons Spice Mix

Spice Mix
Pinch of freshly ground nutmeg
1/2 in (1 cm) cinnamon stick, broken into small pieces
1 teaspoon green cardamom pods
1 tablespoon whole cloves
1 teaspoon peppercorns
1 teaspoon mace blades
4 star anise pods

1 Prepare the Spice Mix first by combining all the spices (without roasting them) and grinding them to a powder in a spice grinder. Set aside.

2 Grind the chickpeas or garbanzo beans and dried chili to a powder in a spice grinder. Process the coconut and peanuts in a food processor until fine. Add the chickpea mixture and process until well combined. Set aside.

3 Heat the oil in a wok over medium heat and stir-fry the sliced onion until golden brown, 5-10 minutes. Add the ground mixture and cook, stirring often, for 5 minutes. Add the salt, coconut milk and water, and mix well. Add the chicken pieces and bring to a simmer. Cover and cook, stirring occasionally, until the chicken is cooked through, 20–30 minutes.

4 Using tongs, remove the chicken pieces from the sauce. Add the yogurt, lemon juice and 4 teaspoons of the Spice Mix to the sauce, mix well and simmer for 5 minutes until heated through, adjusting the taste with more salt as needed. Return the chicken to the pan and mix until well coated. Remove from the heat and serve immediately.

Baked Chicken with Herbs and Spices

1¹/₂ lbs (700 g) boneless chicken thigh meat, each halved
Oil, for greasing
Sprigs of cilantro (coriander leaves), to garnish

Marinade
1 cinnamon stick
1¹/₂ teaspoons green cardamom pods
1¹/₂ teaspoons whole cloves
1 teaspoon peppercorns
¹/₄ cup (10 g) cilantro (coriander leaves)
25 curry leaves
Freshly squeezed juice of ¹/₂ lemon
1-2 green chili peppers
1 in (3 cm) fresh ginger root, peeled and sliced
3 cloves garlic
1¹/₂ teaspoons tamarind concentrate
1 teaspoon ground turmeric
1 teaspoon salt, or to taste

1 Prepare the Marinade first by grinding the cinnamon, cardamom, cloves and peppercorns to a powder in a spice grinder. Combine with all the other ingredients and process to a smooth paste in a food processor or blender. Transfer to a mixing bowl.
2 Place the chicken in the Marinade and mix until well coated. Allow to marinate for 15 minutes.
3 Preheat the oven to 475 °F (240 °C).
4 Lightly grease a large baking sheet with a little oil and arrange the marinated chicken in a single layer. Bake the chicken in the oven, without turning, until cooked through, about 20 minutes. Remove from the heat, garnish with sprigs of cilantro and serve with a salad made of diced onion and sliced spring onion.

Serves 6

Butter Chicken

1 1/2 lbs (700 g) boneless chicken thigh meat, each quartered
3 tablespoons white vinegar or freshly squeezed lemon juice

Marinade
4 tablespoons coriander seeds
1 cinnamon stick, broken into small pieces
3 black cardamom pods
7 green cardamom pods
3/4 teaspoon whole cloves
1 1/2 teaspoons ground turmeric
1 1/2 teaspoons ground red pepper
1 1/2 teaspoons paprika

3/4 teaspoon ground nutmeg
3/4 teaspoon ground mace
3 tablespoons plain yogurt
6 cloves garlic
2 in (5 cm) fresh ginger root, peeled and sliced
1 1/2 tablespoons oil
1 teaspoon salt

Sauce
1/4 cup (60 ml) oil and melted butter combined
2-3 onions, chopped
2 tablespoons grated fresh ginger root
2 tablespoons crushed garlic
1 teaspoon ground red pepper

1 1/2 teaspoons ground turmeric
1 teaspoon chopped green chili peppers
1 lb (500 g) tomatoes, puréed in a blender or one 1-lb (450-g) can stewed tomatoes
3 tablespoons heavy cream
3 tablespoons unsalted melted butter
3 teaspoons honey
1 1/2 tablespoons dried fenugreek leaves
1 teaspoon salt, or to taste
1/4 cup (10 g) chopped cilantro (coriander leaves)

Serves 6

1 Rinse the chicken pieces and drain well. Rub 1 tablespoons of the vinegar or lemon juice into the chicken pieces and set aside.

2 Prepare the Marinade by grinding the coriander seeds, cinnamon, cardamom and cloves to a powder in a spice grinder. Combine with all the other ingredients and the remaining vinegar or lemon juice, and process to a smooth paste in a food processor or blender. Transfer to a mixing bowl. Place the chicken in the Marinade and mix until well coated. Cover and marinate in the refrigerator for 30 minutes.

3 Preheat the oven to 475 °F (240 °C). Lightly grease a shallow roasting pan and arrange the chicken pieces in a single layer. Bake the chicken in the oven, without turning, for about 10 minutes. Remove from the oven and set aside.

4 To make the Sauce, heat the oil and butter mixture in a wok over medium heat and stir-fry the chopped onion, ginger and garlic until fragrant and golden brown, about 10 minutes. Stir in the red pepper, turmeric and chili, and stir-fry for 1 minute. Add the tomato purée and simmer uncovered for 5-10 minutes, stirring often. Add the cream, butter, honey and fenugreek, and mix well. Stir in the baked chicken and simmer until cooked through, about 5 minutes. Season with the salt, add the cilantro and remove from the heat. Serve immediately.

Beef Vindaloo

1/4 cup (60 ml) oil and melted butter combined
3 onions, finely chopped
1 teaspoon salt, or to taste
1 1/2 lbs (700 g) beef, fat trimmed, cubed
Enough water to cover beef
2-3 green chili peppers, slit lengthwise
1/3 cup (85 ml) white vinegar
1/2 teaspoon tamarind concentrate
1/2 teaspoon sugar

Spice Mix
4-5 dried chili peppers, broken into small pieces
1 teaspoon cumin seeds
1 tablespoon peppercorns
1 1/2 tablespoons finely grated fresh ginger root
1 1/2 tablespoons crushed garlic
1/2 teaspoon ground turmeric

1 Prepare the Spice Mix first by grinding the dried chili, cumin seeds and peppercorns to a powder in a spice grinder. Combine with all the other ingredients in a bowl and mix well. Set aside.

2 Heat the oil and butter mixture in a wok over medium heat and stir-fry the onion until golden brown, 10–15 minutes. Stir in the beef, increase the heat to high and stir-fry for about 5 minutes. Add the Spice Mix and continue to stir-fry for 2 minutes until fragrant. Pour in enough water to cover the beef, add the chili and bring to a boil. Reduce the heat to low and simmer partially covered, stirring occasionally, until the sauce is reduced to half, about 1 hour.

3 Season with the vinegar, tamarind, sugar and salt and continue to simmer uncovered for another 20-30 minutes, until the sauce thickens. Remove from the heat and serve hot with steamed rice.

Serves 6

Lamb Biryani

1 lb (500 g) boneless lamb, cut into serving pieces
1 cup (200 g) uncooked basmati rice
1/3 cup (85 ml) oil and melted butter combined
1 1/2 onions, thinly sliced
Freshly squeezed juice of 1/2 lemon

Marinade
1/3 cup (85 ml) plain yogurt
1/3 cup (15 g) chopped cilantro (coriander leaves)
1/3 cup (15 g) chopped mint
1-2 green chili peppers, chopped
2 teaspoons finely grated fresh ginger root

2 teaspoons crushed garlic
2 tablespoons Garam Masala (page 10)
2 teaspoons red chili pepper
2 teaspoons ground turmeric
1 1/2 teaspoons salt
Pinch of saffron, soaked in 2 tablespoons hot milk for 10 minutes

1 Prepare the Marinade first by combining all the ingredients in a large bowl and mixing well. Add the lamb pieces and mix until well coated. Cover and marinate in the refrigerator for at least 1 hour.

2 Place the rice in a bowl and add water to cover. Swirl with your hand, let the rice settle, then drain off the water. Repeat 6-7 times. Add enough water to cover the washed rice and leave to soak for 20 minutes.

3 Heat the oil and butter mixture in a large pot over medium heat and stir-fry the onion until golden brown, about 5 minutes. Add the marinated lamb, increase the heat to high and stir-fry for about 3 minutes. Reduce the heat to low and simmer uncovered for 20-30 minutes until the lamb is tender.

4 Drain the soaked rice and add it to the pot with the lamb, then add enough water just to cover. Mix well and cover the pot tightly. Increase the heat to high and bring the rice mixture to a boil, then reduce the heat and simmer over low heat until the rice is cooked, about 20 minutes. Do not lift the cover when cooking the rice. Remove from the heat and gently stir the cooked rice, then replace the cover and let it stand for 10 minutes before serving. Drizzle the Briyani Rice with lime juice and serve immediately.

Serves 4

Grilled Lamb Chops

2 lbs (1 kg) lamb cutlets
Oil, for brushing
Onion rings, to serve
Mint leaves, to serve
Lemon wedges, to serve

Marinade
1 cinnamon stick
1 teaspoon peppercorns
1 teaspoon finely grated
  fresh ginger root
1 teaspoon crushed garlic
4-6 green chili peppers,
  ground to a paste
$1/_2$ teaspoon salt

1 Prepare the Marinade by grinding the cinnamon and peppercorns to a powder in a spice grinder. Combine with all the other ingredients in a mixing bowl and mix well.

2 Rub the Marinade into both sides of the lamb cutlets and allow to marinate for 30 minutes.

3 Grill the marinated lamb on a preheated pan grill or over a broiler, brushing with a little oil as needed, until cooked to your liking, 3-4 minutes on one side. Arrange the grilled lamb on serving platters, top with the onion rings and mint leaves, and serve with lemon wedges.

Serves 6

Masala Lamb Chops

1/4 cup (60 ml) oil and melted butter combined
2 onions, chopped
2 tablespoons finely grated fresh ginger root
2 tablespoons crushed garlic
3 tablespoons Spice Mix (see below)
2 ripe tomatoes, chopped
4 teaspoons white vinegar
1/2 teaspoon salt
2 lbs (1 kg) lamb chops
Freshly squeezed juice of 1/2 lemon
1 portion Chappati (page 34)

Spice Mix
2 dried chili peppers, broken into small pieces
2 1/2 tablespoons coriander seeds
1 in (3 cm) cinnamon stick, broken into small pieces
1/2 teaspoon peppercorns
1 teaspoon whole cloves
1/2 teaspoon cumin seeds
1/2 teaspoon ground turmeric

1 Prepare the Chappati following the recipe on page 34.
2 To make the Spice Mix, dry-roast all the ingredients in a small pan over low heat until just fragrant, about 5 minutes. Remove from the heat and set aside to cool, then grind to a powder in a spice grinder.
3 Heat the oil and butter mixture in a large heavy saucepan over medium heat and sauté the onion until golden brown, 5-10 minutes. Add the ginger, garlic and 3 tablespoons of the Spice Mix, and sauté until fragrant, about 1 minute. Stir in the chopped tomato and season with the vinegar and salt, adding 1–2 tablespoons of water to the mixture if necessary.
4 Add the lamb and mix to coat it well with the sauce. Reduce the heat to low and simmer uncovered, turning the lamb often, until the lamb is cooked to your liking and sauce is thick, 15–20 minutes. Remove from the heat, drizzle with the lemon juice and serve hot with Chappati.

Serves 6

Lamb Roganjosh Curry

1 lb (500 g) boneless lamb, cubed
1 cup (250 ml) plain yogurt, whisked
1 teaspoon salt, or to taste
$^1/_3$ cup (85 ml) oil and melted butter combined
$^1/_2$ cinnamon stick
10 green cardamom pods
2 black cardamom pods
1 teaspoon whole cloves
2 onions, chopped
1 tablespoon finely grated fresh ginger root
1 tablespoon crushed garlic
2 teaspoons ground red pepper
1 teaspoon ground turmeric
2 tablespoons chopped cilantro (coriander leaves)
1 teaspoon Garam Masala (page 10)

1 In a large bowl, combine the lamb, yogurt and $^1/_2$ teaspoon of the salt, and mix well. Set aside for 10 minutes.

2 Heat the oil and butter mixture in a large skillet over medium heat and sauté the cinnamon, cardamom and cloves until fragrant, about 30 seconds. Add the chopped onion and remaining salt, and sauté until the onion is golden brown, 5–10 minutes. Add the ginger and garlic, and sauté for 30 seconds. Drain off the oil, leaving the onion and spices in the pan.

3 Add the lamb and yogurt mixture, red pepper and turmeric to the pan, and mix well. Reduce the heat to low and simmer covered until the lamb is tender, 45–60 minutes. Stir in the cilantro and Garam Masala, and adjust the taste with more salt if desired. Remove from the heat and serve hot with steamed rice.

You can use goat meat in place of the lamb.

Serves 4

Fresh Curried Crabs

4 lbs (1³/₄ kg) fresh crabs
in shells
1 cup (250 ml) oil and
melted butter combined
1 stick cinnamon
3 green cardamom pods
3 whole cloves
2-3 onions, diced
1¹/₂ tablespoons grated
fresh ginger root
1¹/₂ tablespoons crushed
garlic

3 tablespoons coriander
seeds, ground to a
powder
2-3 teaspoons ground
red pepper
2 teaspoons ground
turmeric
3 ripe tomatoes, finely
chopped, or one 14-oz
(440-g) can chopped
stewed tomatoes

1 teaspoon salt
1 cup (40 g) chopped
cilantro (coriander leaves)
18 curry leaves, torn into
pieces
4 teaspoons crushed
peppercorns

Serves 6

1 Scrub and rinse the crabs well and detach the claws from each crab. Lift off the outer shell and discard. Scrape out any roe and discard the gills.

2 Rinse well and quarter the crabs with a sharp knife. Crack the claws with a mallet. Pat dry with paper towels and set aside.

3 Heat the oil and butter mixture in a wok over medium heat and stir-fry the cinnamon, cardamom and cloves until fragrant, about 30 seconds. Add the onion, ginger and garlic, and stir-fry until golden brown, about 10 minutes. Add the ground coriander, red pepper and turmeric, and stir-fry for 1 minute. Stir in the tomato and simmer, stirring often, until the tomato is soft, about 10 minutes, then season with the salt. Add the crab pieces and mix well. Cover and simmer, turning occasionally, until the crab pieces are just cooked, 10-15 minutes.

4 Using tongs, remove the crab from the pan. Add the remaining ingredients to the sauce in the pan and mix well, adjusting the taste with more salt if desired. Return the crab pieces to the pan and turn to coat them well with the sauce. Remove from the heat and serve immediately.

Fish with Herbs Steamed in Banana Leaf

Four 10-in (25-cm) banana leaf squares, scalded with boiling water until soft, then drained
1 1/2 lbs (700 g) white fish fillets, cut into 4 pieces
Lime wedges, to serve

Coconut Herb Mix
2 cups (200 g) grated fresh coconut
2-3 green chili peppers, coarsely chopped
1/3 cup (15 g) cilantro (coriander leaves)
1/4 cup (10 g) mint
2 tablespoons oil

2 cloves garlic
1/2 teaspoon ground turmeric
1/2 teaspoon cumin seeds
Freshly squeezed juice of 2 limes
1/2 teaspoon sugar
1 teaspoon salt, or to taste

1 Prepare the Coconut Herb Mix by processing all the ingredients in a food processor until fine and dividing it into 4 equal portions. Set aside.

2 To make the fish parcels, place a piece of fish on a banana leaf square. Smear 1 portion of the Coconut Herb Mix over the fish.

3 Fold in the sides of the banana leaf square and fold the edge over the fish. Continue to fold up tightly into a parcel and secure with toothpicks. Make all the other fish parcels with the remaining ingredients in the same manner.

4 Steam the fish parcels in a steamer or in a wok over boiling water until cooked, 12-15 minutes. Remove from the heat, unwrap the fish and serve hot with lime wedges.

If banana leaves are unavailable, you can use parchment or aluminum foil instead.

Makes 4 parcels; serves 4

Crispy Fried Shrimp

1 1/2 lbs (700 g) fresh shrimp, peeled and deveined, tails intact
3/4 cup (130 g) coarse semolina flour
Oil, for deep-frying
1 lemon, cut into wedges, to serve

Marinade
3 tablespoons coriander seeds, ground to a powder
1 1/2 tablespoons oil
3 teaspoons grated fresh ginger root
3 teaspoons crushed garlic
3 teaspoons tamarind concentrate
1 1/2 teaspoons ground red pepper
1 1/2 teaspoons fennel seeds
1 teaspoon ground turmeric
12 curry leaves, finely chopped
1 teaspoon salt, or to taste

1 Combine the Marinade ingredients in a mixing bowl and mix well. Place the shrimp in the Marinade and mix until well coated. Allow to marinate for at least 5 minutes.

2 Fill a wok or saucepan with oil to a depth of 2 in (5 cm) and heat over medium heat to 375 °F (190 °C). In several batches, roll the marinated shrimp in the semolina to coat well, then deep-fry in the hot oil until golden, 1-2 minutes each. Remove from the heat and drain on paper towels. Arrange the shrimp on a serving platter and serve hot with lime wedges.

Serves 4–6

Spicy Portuguese Shrimp

1½ lbs (700 g) fresh
 shrimp, peeled and
 deveined, tails intact
Salt, to taste
2 tablespoons oil
Freshly squeezed juice of
 1 lemon
1 portion Chappati
 (page 34)

Spice Paste
3 dried chili peppers,
 broken into small
 pieces
3 teaspoons peppercorns
1 teaspoon cumin seeds
3 tablespoons white
 vinegar
3 teaspoons crushed garlic
1 teaspoon tamarind
 concentrate
½ teaspoon ground
 turmeric

Serves 6

1 Prepare the Chappati following the recipe on page 34.
2 To make the Spice Paste, grind the dried chili, peppercorns and cumin seeds to a powder in a spice grinder. Combine with all the other ingredients in a bowl and mix well. Set aside for 10–20 minutes before using.
3 Place the shrimp in a mixing bowl, add the Spice Paste and mix until well coated. Allow to marinate for at least 5 minutes.
4 Heat the oil in a skillet over medium heat until hot. In several batches, fry the marinated shrimp, turning once, until browned, 1–2 minutes. Remove from the heat and drain on paper towels. Arrange the shrimp on serving platters, drizzle with the lemon juice and serve hot with the Chappati.

For a variation, lightly brush the shrimp with the Spice Paste and cook them in batches as above, then set aside. In a small saucepan, heat 2 tablespoons of oil over medium heat and stir-fry 15 curry leaves—or as many as desired—until fragrant, about 30 seconds. Drain the curry leaves on paper towels and toss them with the shrimp. If desired, add thinly sliced red onion for color.

Goan Fish Curry

$1/3$ cup (85 ml) oil and melted butter combined
2 onions, sliced
2 large tomatoes, quartered
1-2 green chili peppers, slit lengthwise
2 cups (500 ml) coconut milk
1 teaspoon salt, or to taste
$1^1/2$ lbs (700 g) white fish fillets, cut into serving pieces

Spice Paste
12 dried chili peppers, broken into small pieces
4 tablespoons coriander seeds
3 tablespoons cumin seeds
$1/2$ cup (125 ml) white vinegar
2 teaspoons grated fresh ginger root
2 teaspoons crushed garlic
$1^1/2$ teaspoons ground turmeric

1 Prepare the Spice Paste first by grinding the dried chili, coriander seeds and cumin seeds to a powder in a spice grinder. Combine with all the other ingredients in a bowl and mix well. Set aside.

2 Heat the oil in a wok over medium heat and stir-fry the onion until golden brown, about 5 minutes. Add the Spice Paste and stir-fry until fragrant, about 3 minutes. Stir in the tomato, chili and coconut milk, and bring to a simmer. Cook, stirring often, until the tomato is soft, about 5 minutes. Season with the salt. Add the fish and continue to simmer uncovered until the fish is cooked, about 5 minutes. Remove from the heat and serve hot with steamed rice.

Serves 4–6

Fish Curry with Tomato and Coconut

1 1/2 lbs (700 g) white fish fillets
3 tablespoons oil
1 teaspoon mustard seeds
1/2 teaspoon fenugreek seeds
3 dried chili peppers
2 medium onions, thinly sliced
2 tablespoons grated fresh ginger root
2 tablespoons crushed garlic
36 curry leaves
3 teaspoons ground turmeric
2 tablespoons ground red pepper
2 ripe tomatoes, coarsely chopped
1 1/2 cups (375 ml) coconut cream
1 teaspoon tamarind concentrate
1 teaspoon salt, or to taste
Freshly squeezed juice of 1/2 lemon

1 Rinse the fish well. Remove the skin and sliced into bite-sized pieces.

2 Heat the oil in a wok over medium heat and stir-fry the mustard seeds until they crackle, about 30 seconds. Add the fenugreek and dried peppers, and stir-fry until fragrant, about 30 seconds. Add the sliced onion, ginger and garlic, and stir-fry until golden brown, about 5 minutes. Add the curry leaves, turmeric and ground pepper, and mix well, then stir in the chopped tomato. Simmer uncovered for about 3 minutes until the tomato is soft. Pour in the coconut cream and season with the tamarind and salt.

3 Add the fish to the curry, cover and simmer until the fish is just cooked through, about 5 minutes. Stir in the lemon juice and remove from the heat. Serve hot with steamed rice.

Serves 6

Pistachio Kulfi Ice Cream

Large pinch of saffron threads	3 tablespoons ground green cardamom	**Star Anise Sauce**
$^1/_2$ cup (125 ml) milk, heated	$1^2/_3$ cups (400 ml) condensed milk	$^1/_2$ cup (100 g) sugar
$^1/_3$ cup (100 g) pistachio nuts, finely chopped	3 cups (750 ml) heavy cream	$^1/_2$ cup (125 ml) heavy cream
		5 star anise pods

1 Combine the saffron and hot milk in a bowl and set aside for 10 minutes.

2 Combine the condensed milk and cream in a bowl and stir well; do not whisk or beat. Add the chopped pistachio, saffron mixture and ground cardamom and mix until well blended. Pour the mixture equally into 10 ramekins (each $^1/_2$-cup/125-ml capacity), then freeze in the freezer for about 6 hours.

3 Meanwhile prepare the Sauce by heating all the ingredients in a small pan over medium heat, stirring, until all the sugar is dissolved. Reduce the heat to low and simmer uncovered until the Sauce is thick, about 10 minutes. Remove from the heat.

4 To serve, briefly dip each ramekin in a bowl of hot water. Place a serving platter over the ramekin and invert the ice cream onto the serving platter. Spread 1 teaspoon of the Sauce on top of the ice cream and serve immediately.

Makes 10 small servings

Mango Kulfi Ice Cream

1 ripe mango (about 12 oz/350 g), peeled, pitted and coarsely chopped
1 1/2 tablespoons green cardamom pods ground to a powder, or 2 teaspoons cardamom powder

1 2/3 cups (400 ml) condensed milk
3 cups (750 ml) heavy cream
1 portion Star Anise Sauce (opposite page), to serve
Mango slices, to garnish

Makes 10 small servings

You can make these ice creams up to 2 weeks ahead. Wrap the ice cream well to prevent it from absorbing the flavors from other foods in the freezer. Make the Sauce close to serving.

1 Process the mango flesh until smooth in a food processor or blender. Combine with the cardamom and mix well.

2 Combine the condensed milk, cream and mango mixture in a bowl and stir until well blended; do not whisk or beat. Pour the mixture equally into 10 ramekins (each 1/2-cup/125-ml capacity), then freeze in the freezer for about 6 hours.

3 Meanwhile, make the Star Anise Sauce following the recipe on the opposite page.

4 Briefly dip each ramekin in a bowl of hot water. Place a serving platter over the ramekin and invert the ice cream onto the serving platter. Garnish with mango slices and serve immediately with a bowl of the Star Anise Sauce on the side.

Gulab Jamun
(Cottage Cheese Dumplings in Syrup)

Oil, for deep-frying

Syrup
2 cups (400 g) sugar
2 cups (500 ml) water
1 green cardamom pod, cracked
Small pinch of saffron threads

Dumplings
1 cup (90 g) milk powder
$^1/_2$ cup (75 g) flour, sifted
Pinch of ground cardamom
$^1/_2$ cup (125 ml) heavy cream

Serves 4

1 Prepare the Syrup first by combining all the ingredients in a saucepan. Heat the mixture over low heat, stirring often, until the sugar is dissolved. Keep the Syrup warm over very low heat.

2 To make the Dumplings, combine the milk, flour and cardamom in a mixing bowl. Gradually add the cream, mixing with your fingers until the mixture turns into a soft dough. Knead the dough in the bowl until smooth.

3 Divide the dough into 10 equal portions and shape each portion into a walnut-sized ball. If necessary, lightly brush the dough balls with a little water to avoid drying out. Cover with a cloth.

4 Fill a wok or large saucepan with oil and heat over medium heat to 350 °F (180 °C). In several batches, deep-fry the Dumplings, turning often, until golden brown on all sides, 3–4 minutes. Remove from the heat and drain on paper towels. Drop the deep-fried Dumplings in the warm Syrup and soak for at least 30 minutes. Serve warm.

Always serve two or more Gulab Jamun per guest as it is considered rude to offer only one.

Chilled Sweet Lassi Yogurt Drink

Pinch of saffron threads
$1/_3$ cup (85 ml) milk,
  heated
$1^1/_2$ tablespoons green
  cardamom pods
  ground to a powder, or
  2 teaspoons ground
  cardamom
4 cups (1 liter) plain
  yogurt
$1/_4$ cup (60 g) powdered
  (castor) sugar
Crushed ice, to serve

1 Combine the saffron and hot milk in a bowl and set aside for 10 minutes.

2 In a jug, combine all the ingredients, except the crushed ice, and whisk thoroughly until the sugar is dissolved and the drink begins to froth. Pour into serving glasses, add some crushed ice and serve immediately.

You can thin the lassi by adding more milk.

Serves 4

Green Mango Juice

1 lb (500 g) unripe green mangoes
1 1/2 tablespoons green cardamom pods ground to a powder, or 2 teaspoons cardamom powder
1/4 cup (50 g) sugar
Pinch of salt
4 cups (1 liter) iced water
Crushed ice, to serve

Serves 4

1 Rinse the mangoes well and place in a large saucepan. Add enough water to cover and bring to a boil over medium heat. Simmer, partially covered, until the mangoes are soft, 20–30 minutes. Remove from the heat, drain and reserve the cooking water. Allow the mangoes to cool.
2 Peel the mangoes and remove the mango pulp from the pits. Discard the skins and pits. Process the mango pulp with the cardamom, sugar and salt until smooth, adding some cooking water if necessary. Combine the mango purée with the iced water in a jar, adjusting the taste with more sugar and salt as needed. Pour into tall glasses, add some crushed ice and serve immediately.

For a variation, omit the cardamom and add 1/2 teaspoon of ground, dry-roasted cumin seeds and a handful of fresh mint leaves.

Cardamon Lemon Juice

1 teaspoon ground car-
damom
4 cups (1 liter) iced water
Freshly squeezed juice of
3 lemons or 5 limes
3 tablespoons powdered
(castor) sugar, or to
taste
$1/_2$ teaspoon salt, or to
taste
Crushed ice, to serve

Combine all the ingredients, except the crushed ice, in a jar and whisk until the sugar is dissolved. Pour into tall glasses, add some crushed ice and serve immediately.

Serves 4

Chai Milk Tea

4 cups (1 liter) water
4 teaspoons finely grated
  fresh ginger root
$1/_3$ cup (30 g) tea leaves
3 tablespoons milk, plus
  extra milk to serve
$1/_2$ teaspoon Garam
  Masala (page 10)
Sugar, to taste

Serves 4

1 Bring the water and ginger to a boil over medium heat in a saucepan. Reduce the heat to low, stir in the tea leaves and return to a boil. Add the milk and Garam Masala and mix well. Remove from the heat.
2 Cover the pan and set aside for about 5 minutes. Strain and add sugar to taste. Serve hot with extra milk.

Indians generally drink their Chai strong with lots of milk and sugar, but you can vary the amounts depending on your taste. As a variation, use ground cardamom instead of the Garam Masala.

Complete List of Recipes